This
PJ BOOK
belongs to
PJ Library
JEWISH BEDTIME STORIES and SONGS

To Naomi, who persevered —L.K.
To Grandma Ronnie, who doodled —T.S.

Visit us on the Web! randomhousekids.com

Educators and librarians, for a variety of teaching tools, visit us at RHTeachersLibrarians.com

ISBN: 978-0-375-97312-3

MANUFACTURED IN MALAYSIA
10 9 8 7 6 5 4 3 2 1
First Edition

Random House Children's Books supports the First Amendment and celebrates the right to read.

041525K1/B482

Everybody Says Shalom

by Leslie Kimmelman
illustrated by Talitha Shipman

RANDOM HOUSE NEW YORK

Gili the Gecko says, "In Israel, *shalom* is how people say hello. *Shalom* is also how people say goodbye. But its first and most important meaning is 'peace.' It's a little word with a lot to say!"

When in Israel . . . everybody says *shalom*!

Going out . . .
. . . or coming home.

Right to left
and left to right.

In the morning . . .

שביל הנחש
SNAKE PATH

late at night.

With a tune.

On a dune.

Eating yogurt with a spoon.

Everybody says *shalom*,
in a *shuk* . . .

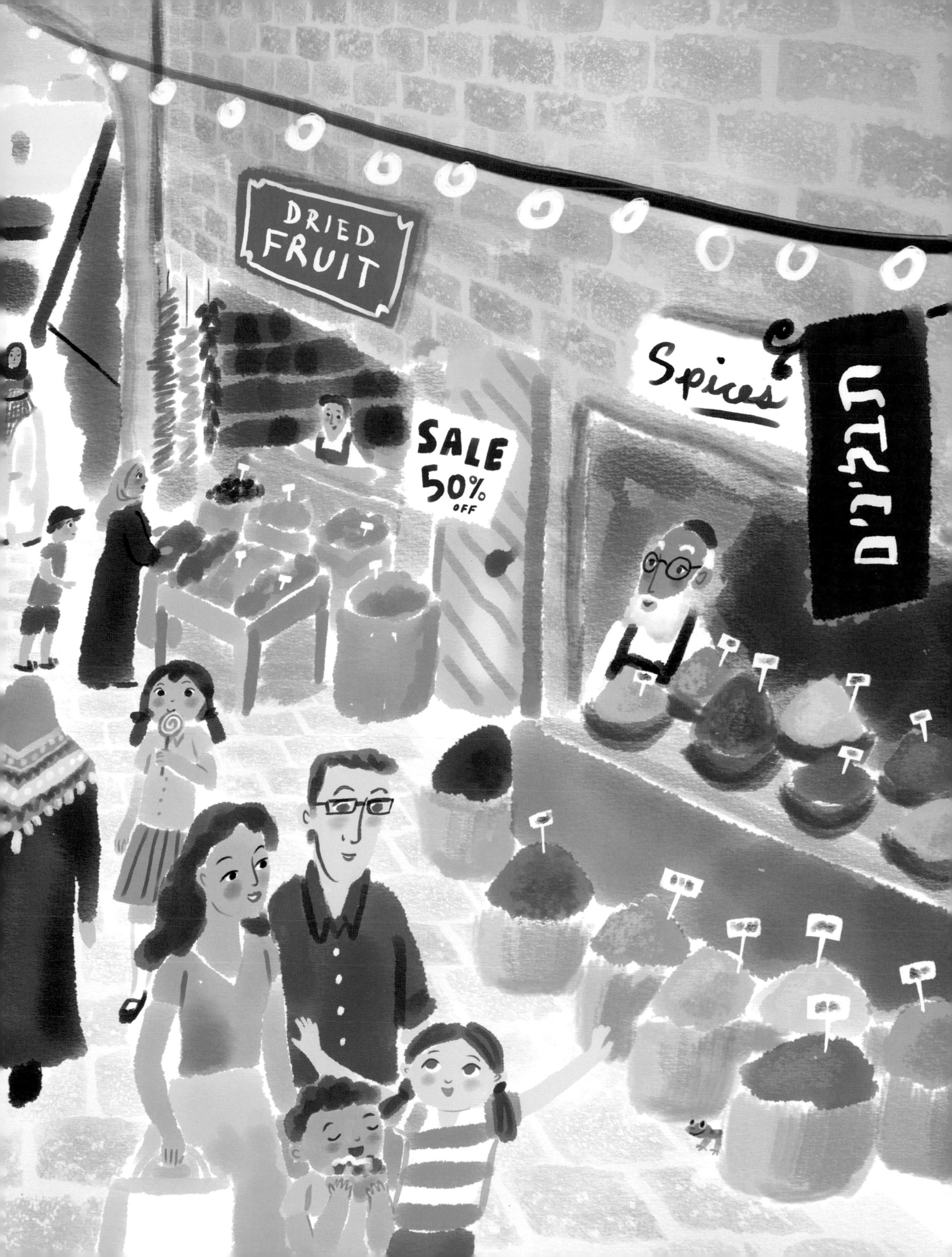

DRIED FRUIT

SALE 50% OFF

Spices

. . . or catacomb.

Two by two,
in the zoo.

Viewing tiny tiles of blue.

Munching dates,

lifting crates.

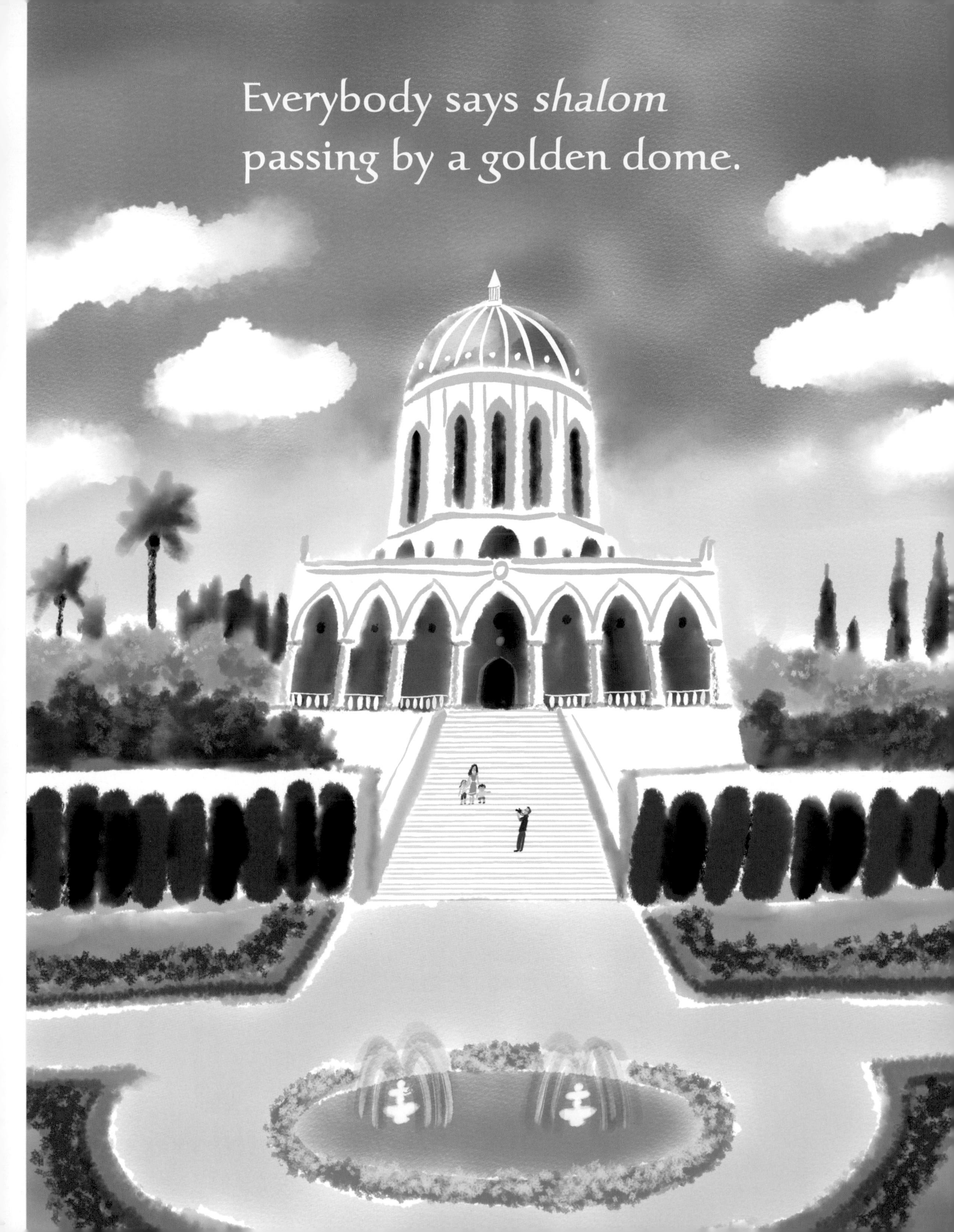

Everybody says *shalom*
passing by a golden dome.

Gazing.

Grazing.

Fishing.

Wishing.

Floating.

Boating.

Haying.

Praying.

Everybody says *shalom.*
Shalom, Israel.
Heading home.

Around and About in Israel

Masada is a fortress that was built way back in ancient times, on the edge of the Judean Desert and high up on a rock cliff overlooking the Dead Sea. Jews fled there to try to keep themselves safe from Roman soldiers. Today, visitors can climb to the top on the twisty Snake Path. They can also ride up in a cable car.

A **shuk** (*souk* in Arabic), or open-air market, can be found in almost every city in Israel. The shops and stalls that crowd its alleyways are fragrant with the smells of spices and foods of all kinds. Try some fresh dates, or falafel, or locally caught fish, or challah and pita bread right from the oven.

Catacombs are long, winding underground tunnels and large caves that were used long ago to bury the dead. Some of them contain beautiful mineral formations—stalactites hanging from the ceilings and stalagmites rising from the ground. Look for interesting carvings in the walls.

Jerusalem's **Biblical Zoo** has more than 170 kinds of animals, many of which are mentioned in the Bible. Its visitor center is shaped like Noah's Ark—to show the zoo's commitment to protecting endangered species.

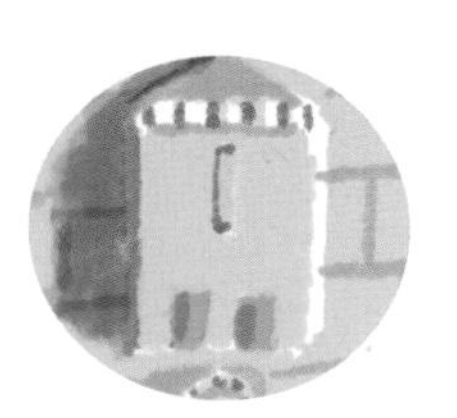

Eight gates surround the Old City of Jerusalem, seven of which are still in use. The Jaffa Gate, one of the busiest entrances to the Old City, faces what was once the main route to the port of Jaffa. Nearby is the Tower of David, a very old part of the city walls. The Lion's Gate is named for the fierce-looking animals carved in its stone—though many people think they are leopards or tigers. The New Gate is not very new—it's over a hundred years old!—but it *is* newer than the other gates.

The **Baha'i Shrine** on Mount Carmel, in Haifa, is one of the holiest places on earth for people of the Baha'i faith. Its spectacular gardens draw visitors from around the world. With its golden dome, made of more than twelve thousand tiles, the shrine is one of many such buildings found in Israel. Jerusalem's holy and iconic gold-topped Dome of the Rock, one of the oldest works of Islamic architecture, is another.

The **Chagall Windows** can be found in Hadassah Medical Center in Jerusalem. Marc Chagall, a Jewish artist who was born in Belarus (then part of the Russian Empire), gave these beautiful stained-glass windows to the medical center in 1962. He was inspired by the Bible's story of the blessings that Jacob gave his sons, whose descendants became the twelve tribes of Israel.

The **Dead Sea** is so salty that you float in it without even trying! It's called the Dead Sea because the water is too salty for any fish to live in it. Dead Sea mud is thought to be good for your skin, so some people like to rub it all over their bodies.

The **Red Sea** teems with marine life, including dolphins, sharks, and over a thousand other kinds of fish.

A **kibbutz** is a community living and working together, organized like a village. The kibbutz provides education, food, and other things the community needs, including social activities and entertainment. It used to be that people on kibbutzim (the plural of *kibbutz*) mainly farmed the land and raised animals. Today, many kibbutzim have factories that make industrial and high-tech products.

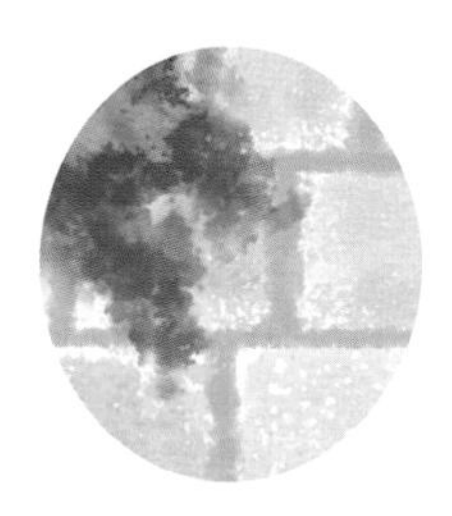

The **Western Wall**, or **Kotel** (pronounced KO-tell), is the most important remnant of the ancient Second Temple in Jerusalem. Jewish people from all over the world come to this holy place to pray. Many write their prayers and hopes on small pieces of paper to tuck into crevices in the wall. The wall is Judaism's holiest site. Jerusalem is also a holy place for Christians and Muslims.